Contents

1 The Tudor countryside

In Tudor times, all kinds of people lived in the country – rich **nobles**, **gentlemen**, **traders** of all kinds, and **beggars** too. But most people worked on the land – farmers, the **labourers** who worked for them, and their families. Between 1485 and 1603 (the Tudor period) the population of England roughly doubled. There were more people everywhere. More people were trying to make a living from farming. There were many more people travelling the countryside looking for work.

This page shows a survey map, made in 1591, of the manor of Feckenham, Worcestershire.

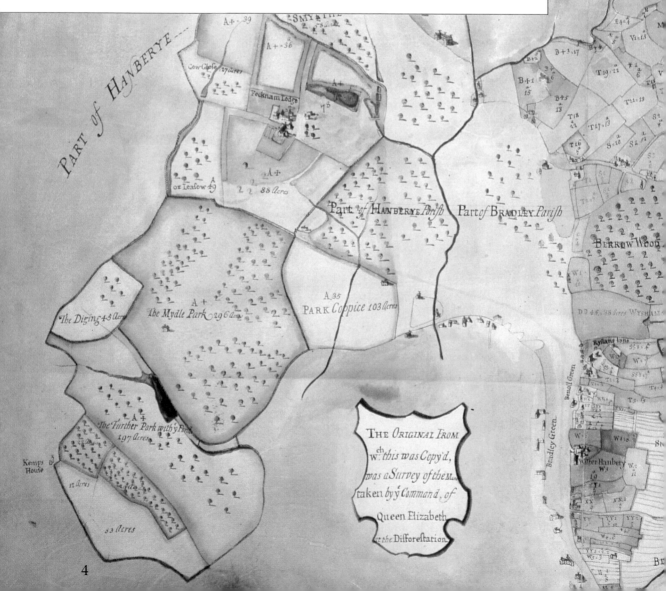

The map of Feckenham used in this unit was chosen because it shows many important features of country living between 1485 and 1603. All the land on the map belonged to the lord of the **manor**. People rented land from him, or worked on his land in return for a house to live in and some land to farm for themselves. Some of the land was used for growing crops, some was used for **grazing** animals. There was also woodland nearby.

Survey maps like this show how the land was used and who rented the various pieces of land. The letters refer to the names of the **tenants**.

Source A

The soil here is better for feeding and grazing animals than it is for growing corn. So there are a great many cattle in our country, and sheep also. Nowadays there is scarcely a quarter of the land that is used for growing grain of any sort.

Written in 1577, by William Harrison in his book, *A Description of England*. Many foreigners who visited England between 1485 and 1603 marvelled at the huge numbers of grazing animals, as well as their size.

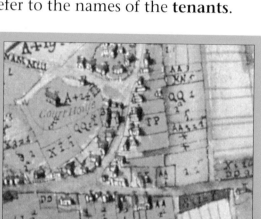

Feckenham town

The workers of Feckenham relied on the local countryside for work. They all traded with local people. Feckenham had a **miller**, a butcher and a **blacksmith**. It probably had a baker, a carpenter and at least one person who could mend wheels and farming machinery. It had at least one **alehouse** selling beer brewed by the owner. There was a church and a **clergyman**. Towns of this size often had **tailors**, shoemakers and **potters**, too.

Feckenham Lodge

Feckenham Lodge was the manor house. The family who owned the whole manor might have lived there. If the manor was owned by a rich noble (living in a grander house somewhere else), the manor house was rented to a rich gentleman, or to one of the poorer members of the noble's family. Feckenham Lodge had gardens, a private park and private woods. It also had **fishponds** that were made by moving the river.

The mill

Mills ground up wheat or barley to make flour, mostly used for bread. Mills built beside rivers, like the one at Feckenham, were powered by water. Other mills were built in windy places. Their **sails** caught the wind and turned. The turning sails powered the machinery inside.

Strip farming

In 1485 most farming was done by dividing the big fields of the manor up into strips. Different farmers were given different strips in each field. This meant that each farmer had some of the best land and some of the rest. There were also big fields called 'common fields' that everyone used to graze their animals on. Everyone had to do big jobs, like ploughing, at the same time, and had to grow the same crops in each field.

Enclosed fields

From 1485 there was a move away from strip farming. Some farmers joined several strips together, often putting a fence or hedge around the land to **enclose** it. This worked if everyone agreed to enclose and a fair division was made. But there were problems when rich landowners enclosed fields and **common land**. It was worse if they stopped growing crops and changed to keeping sheep. They needed fewer workers and so turned tenants out of their homes.

Big houses

Some farmers did well out of enclosing land. They could rent more fields and do even better. They built new, bigger houses. Some of these were so big that they were marked on survey maps with the owner's name, like John Grant (his fields are marked with 'E' and then a number on the map).

2 Lady Grace Mildmay 1552–1620

Lady Grace Mildmay, like the wives of many nobles, spent her life in the country while her husband was at **Court**. We know about her life because she left an **autobiography** and other papers, which have survived to the present day.

Childhood and marriage

Grace was the middle daughter of Sir Henry Sharington. She was married to Anthony Mildmay in 1567. The marriage was arranged by their families. Grace was about fifteen, Anthony was about twenty. Grace seemed to accept the marriage. Anthony complained bitterly about it.

Anthony and Grace went to live with Anthony's parents at Apethorpe, Northamptonshire. Sir Walter Mildmay was rich, but only gave them a small amount to live on. Grace admits this 'could not keep us, as my husband was often serving the Queen either at Court or as an **ambassador** abroad'. Sir Walter and his son were more often at Court than at home.

Grace's father-in-law, Sir Walter Mildmay. 'He was ready to do every man good and hurt no man,' said Grace, 'and his wife was a virtuous and dutiful wife.' Grace and Anthony depended on Sir Walter for a place to live, wages for servants, even food and drink. Grace and Lady Mary Mildmay lived together at Apethorpe while their husbands were at Court.

Source A

Sir Walter's son, being then more willing to travel to get experience of the world than to marry so soon, did not wish to marry me. His father told him if he did not marry me, then he would marry no-one.

From Lady Grace Mildmay's autobiography.

Source B

Country life

Anthony and Grace had only one child, Mary, born in 1582. By the time Mary was born, Grace had been living at Apethorpe for fifteen years. She had a country life routine. She ran the house, read the Bible, prayed and cared for the sick. For entertainment she sang, played the **lute** and embroidered. She did not run the estate in Anthony's absence, as some **noble** ladies did for their husbands. The Mildmay men **hired** a man to do this job. Grace did not have anything to do with the village people, other than the servants or the people who came to her because they were sick.

Grace had little to do with bringing up her daughter, who is hardly mentioned in Grace's autobiography. This may be partly because she had given up hoping to have a child – most nobles had their first children quickly – one a year was common. Mary had to fit into Grace's set routine. When Mary was married in 1599, life at Apethorpe went on as usual. Sir Anthony died in 1617. Lady Grace died three years later. In her **will** she left money to pay for services to be held yearly in the local church, and for someone to teach the local children to read and write.

A typical life?

In some ways Lady Grace was a typical **courtier's** wife. She stayed in the country, her husband went to Court. She had a full and busy life running a home and caring for the sick, like other noble wives.

But Grace did not have her own home (until Sir Walter died in 1589) and she had few friends. She had fewer children, later in life, than other noble ladies. She spent more time studying medicine than most ladies, who simply learned enough about herbs to help with minor ailments. Grace produced medicines in large quantities and wrote to several doctors, swapping **cures**.

Source C

The tomb of Lady Grace and Sir Anthony Mildmay, set up in 1621 by their daughter Mary, who was by then married to the Earl of Westmorland.

3 Villagers

Village trades

Some village **trades** were more widespread than others. Almost every village had a blacksmith, baker, miller and carpenter. These were the trades with the closest links to farming. Other trades were more concerned with providing villagers with food or clothing – **tailors**, boot and shoemakers, butchers and **alehouse** keepers. They were most likely to be found in larger villages or small towns.

Just one job?

In larger villages a person could make a living doing just one job, because enough people needed their carts mended, shoes to wear, or meat to eat. In smaller villages people often had several jobs. For example, a butcher might run an alehouse, while someone else mended wheels, made barrels and built houses. Most villagers, even **clergymen**, helped in the fields at harvest time.

Source A

Electricity had not been invented in Tudor times. Candles were expensive so, once it was dark, most people lit their homes with rushes dipped in fat. The rushlight shown here had a handle so it could be carried about.

Improving fortunes: the Finchams	Declining fortunes: the Aldridges
Christopher Fincham, the son of a local **labourer**, was apprenticed to the cooper (barrel-maker) of Terling in 1599. He worked hard and eventually inherited his master's business. He took on other types of carpentry, including making carts. Christopher married a local girl and rented a house in the village. By 1610 he had at least one son and was rich enough to buy some land and build himself a house. He may have had other children, but it is not clear. When he died, he left the house, land and his tools to Thomas, his son. Thomas, also a carpenter, was very successful. He bought more land and became an important person in the village.	John Aldridge and his wife, Susan, had three sons, Thomas, William and John. He was a carpenter and, in 1595, he had his own house and land. He was an important person in the village. When John died, Susan married Thomas Holman, an alehouse-keeper. He was not a good choice. He was often arrested for fighting or for allowing fights to break out in his alehouse. William and Thomas left his care as soon as they could. John farmed the land his father had left and ran an alehouse like his step-father. They both made just enough money to scrape by. Neither was important in the village. When Holman died, Susan ended up living in poverty.

This is an early Tudor illustration of a **saint** working as a **blacksmith**. It shows a blacksmith's tools and forge accurately.

Good neighbours?

It was important that people in the villages all got along with each other reasonably well. They all depended on each other much of the time. This does not mean that they all got on well all of the time. They often formed different groups, linked by family ties and friendships. People who were in the same trade could be good friends or rivals. People of the same level of importance tended to stick together. The most important people in the village were not likely to be friendly with the farm labourers.

Bad neighbours

Various court records show that all villages had regular fights, arguments and thefts. Sometimes these happened because of trade rivalry, sometimes because of personal dislike. Whatever the reason, it is clear that village life was not all peace and quiet!

The Sampford feud

Family quarrels could grow as villagers took sides. In 1565, in Willingdale Doe, Essex, Thomas Sampford fell out with his brother Richard and Richard's wife, Ellen. They accused him of stealing sheep to sell to butchers. They were supported by the Cowland family (whose sheep had been stolen) and a butcher from a nearby village. Thomas said Richard should cut Ellen's throat 'to quieten her'.

The charges were not proved but bad feeling simmered. It broke out six months later, when there was a fight in the churchyard. Richard hit Thomas and Agnes, his wife, with his staff. Richard Bright came to help Thomas. Richard stabbed Bright. Ellen then joined in, pulling out a bit of Thomas' beard and 'striking him on the head with a leg of mutton'. She was fined 12d.

4 Farmers

Different sorts of farmer

The word 'farmer' meant a man with a big farm and many animals. It also meant a man with a small farm and a few sheep. So a man who grew enough to feed his family and one who grew enough to feed half of London were both farmers. A farmer could own or rent his farm.

Different sorts of farm

Different parts of England and Wales were farmed in different ways. Weather and soil had a big effect on this. Marshland and high hills were good for **grazing** sheep, but bad for growing crops. Other places, like the Midlands, Essex and Kent, were good for farming anything.

Between 1485 and 1603 many farmers turned strip fields into enclosed fields. Some farmers changed from growing crops to keeping sheep. Some farmers were forced out of their farms to make way for sheep. They lost their jobs and their homes. Many **labourers** also lost their jobs. The rise in the population meant there were more people looking for farm work just when there was less farm work to be had. The numbers of poor people and beggars in the country rose sharply.

Growing crops was hard work in Tudor times without any machines. Tools like these were used to prune fruit trees and cut back hedges.

The farming year

A farmer who kept animals and grew crops had to get all these things done in the year:

Autumn: pick fruit, sow winter wheat and barley, plough other land. Make sure there is winter **provision** for animals. Thresh grain as needed.

Winter: early on, kill pigs and cattle that cannot be fed through winter. Mend tools and buildings, tend early lambs and calves. Chop firewood, mend fences, barns and hedges.

Spring: plough and sow oats, wheat and barley. Put animals out to grass. Shear sheep.

Summer: second ploughing. Haymaking of first crop. Harvest time was the busiest time of year. Wheat, oats and barley need harvesting at the same time as **flax** and **hemp**. Animals grazed on the **stubble**.

Source A

Source B

This engraving is from Raphael Holinshed's *Chronicles*, printed in 1577. The farmer is well off. He is well dressed and is not helping with the harvest, just giving orders.

Two farms in the 1560s

The information comes from the farmers' inventories.

Robert Hartreige

Robert Hartreige farmed Vinters Farm. He **leased** the farm. The lease was worth £2.

When he died he had:

wheat (in barn)	£2		
peas and hay (in barn)	£1	6s	8d
2 horses	£3		
2 cows, 3 calves	£4	3s	4d
13 acres of wheat	£8	13s	4d
3 pigs		6s	8d
poultry		5s	
tools and carts		18s	6d
Total worth:	**£20**	**13s**	**6d**

Simon Austrey

Simon Austrey farmed Provender Farm. He owned the lease, worth £20.

When he died he had:

wheat (in barns)	£14	13s	
peas and hay (in barns)	£3	6s	2d
oats (in barns)	£2	14s	
barley	£5		
8 horses, harnesses etc.	£23		
cows and calves	£14	7s	2d
38 acres of wheat	£32		
6 acres of oats	£2		
17 acres of peas	£13	6s	8d
24 acres of barley	£11	4s	
29 pigs	£4	5s	
ewes and lambs	£22	5s	4d
poultry		16s	4d
tools and carts	£4	5s	
Total worth:	**£163**	**2s**	**6d**

5 Farmers' wives

What did a farmer's wife do?

The farmer's wife was vital to the running of a Tudor farm. Every farmer needed a woman to run the home. If a farmer did not have a wife, a female relative or a housekeeper lived with him. She was responsible for running the house, feeding the family and the workers, feeding the animals and growing as much of the family food as possible. She also made butter and cheese, and spun and wove wool. Some farmers' wives kept bees to make honey.

Other jobs

As well as the daily jobs, the farmer's wife had other jobs that varied with the farming year. She brewed beer regularly. At harvest time she helped in the fields. This was an especially busy time of year, because she also made jams from wild and home-grown fruits. In the autumn, the farmers killed the pigs they could not feed. The farmer's wife salted joints of pork to preserve them, made sausages and hung joints of meat in the chimney to be preserved by the smoke from the fire. On a large farm, she would have servants to help her.

Source A

Rise early and first sweep the house and get all things in order. Then milk the cows, feed the calves and take the milk to the dairy. Wake and dress the children and make breakfast also for your husband, the children and the servants.

Then you should bake, brew and make sure corn and malt have gone to the mill. You must make cheese and butter whenever you find the time. Pigs should be fed morning and evening, chickens in the morning only.

You must also tend to your garden. Plant many good seeds and herbs and grow things for the pot that are good to eat. You need also to allow time for spinning and weaving woollen cloth.

Instructions to the farmer's wife, from Anthony Fitzherbert's *Book of Husbandry*, a farming book first printed in 1523.

Source B

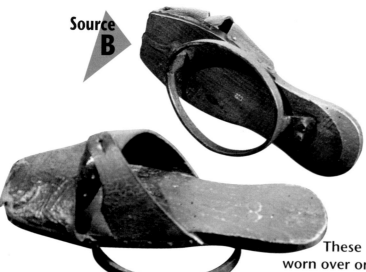

These shoes are called pattens. They were worn over ordinary shoes. The soles were raised off the ground, so the wearer could cross dirty and muddy areas, like a farmyard, without getting their shoes wet and dirty.

Off to market

The farmer's wife went to the weekly **markets** in the nearby towns, to sell any butter, cheese or eggs she had to spare. She also sold vegetables, honey and fruit, and chickens that were too old to lay eggs.

Going to market was also a social occasion. Women met along the way and travelled together. It was safer in groups, and they could catch up on the local news. Each woman sold her goods or **traded** them for things that she wanted. If she sold everything quickly she might go home early, but the markets usually took all day.

A farmer's wife taking live birds to market. They were usually sold live, even if they were to be eaten rather than kept for eggs. This was partly to keep them fresh. Also, their feathers were used for pillows, and chickens are easier to pluck when they have just died and are still warm.

6 Farm labourers

Who were they?

Farm **labourers** worked for farmers. Some labourers worked in return for a cottage to live in and land of their own to farm. Others worked for wages and rented the cottage and land. Others had no permanent jobs or homes and wandered around the country looking for work. Some well-off labourers were better off than farmers, who had higher rents to find and their farms to run. Most labourers just scraped by, earning and growing enough to live on.

Farmers who could not make a living had to sell their farms and become labourers. Sometimes a labourer saved up for a farm, or married a farmer's daughter or widow and became a farmer. But farmers and labourers all did the same jobs, all tied in to the farming year. They had to be able to do any farm job – caring for animals, ploughing, planting, harvesting, shearing sheep, mending walls and hedges, clearing ponds and ditches, and tending orchards.

Wages and prices

Wages for labourers in Tudor times varied depending on the time or season, the place and the generosity of their employer. The rough guide below is based on the average wages offered to a labourer **hired** by the day in southern England. Farmers paid more per day at harvest time, when labourers were expected to work longer hours. Sometimes they fed the labourers, sometimes not. This made a real difference to the value of the labourers' wages.

1485
Daily wage	4d
Loaf of bread	1d
A chicken	1d
A mug of beer	5d

1603
Daily wage	8d
Loaf of bread	4d
A chicken	5d
A mug of beer	2.5d

Source A

This is part of a table carpet, used as a table covering, and it shows a shepherd scaring a wolf away from his sheep.

Source B

September, from a Flemish calendar printed in 1540. The labourer at the front is ploughing, and is followed by a labourer sowing winter wheat or rye. The seeds are then covered by a harrow. The men in the wood are knocking down acorns to feed the pigs. The farmhouse and its garden are on the right of the picture.

7 Other country work

Most people who lived in the countryside worked on the land. But there were other jobs, too.

Fishing

Some fishermen lived and worked in the larger ports around the coast. But there were also lots of tiny villages where people made their living by fishing and selling their catch to the people in the nearby countryside.

Industry in the country

Many **industries** were based in the countryside, where there was water, wood and coal. There were no factories with hundreds of workers. There were small groups of people all working at the same job. Often iron, coal and stone were mined by families who paid the landowners, either in money or by giving them a share of what they mined.

Sometimes landowners ran the mines and **hired** miners to do the work. Elizabeth, Countess of Shrewsbury, did this, as did the Sidney family, who ran the largest **ironworks** in the country at the time. The Sidney ironworks were unusual because they could afford the latest type of furnace, which heated the iron far more quickly. They also employed a lot of workers. This meant that they made a lot of iron and a lot of profit. Most industries were on a smaller scale, making far less profit.

Source A

4 to 11 October

Worth of coal cut	45s	
Paid to pickman	7s	6d
Paid to barrower	2s	6d
Paid to bankman	3s	9d
Candles for barrower		8d
Candles for pickman	1s	3d
Total	**15s**	**8d**
Coal unsold as yet	30s	

From the accounts of a small coal mine outside Sheffield in the 1560s. Pickmen cut the coal, barrowers collected it and took it to the bottom of the shaft. Bankmen lifted the coal to the surface.

Source B

Stoneworkers' tools. People quarried stone, lead or coal all over the country, again on a small scale. Most quarries were worked by one or two families. These tools come from Victorian times, but Tudor tools looked just the same.

Part-time work

Not everyone worked full-time in industries. About two-thirds of all farm workers did part-time work in whatever industry was closest. Some of them worked in quarries or in the iron industry. Others worked from home, either on a very small scale for themselves or for an employer.

Men carved wood. Women did spinning, knitting or basket-making. Some labourers and their families who lived near forests collected and sold wood, or burnt charcoal for the local ironworks.

What did they do?

Part-time work was different in different parts of the country. Some examples include:

Buckinghamshire	making lace
Cornwall	making rush mats
Dorset	making gloves
East Anglia	spinning
Warwickshire	spinning

Salt was expensive. It could be obtained from sea water, by boiling it, or dug out of the ground. This picture from the Netherlands, painted in the 1480s, shows workers boiling sea water to obtain salt. The English made salt like this too.

Source C

8 Marriage and family life

Landowners

Rich landowners and **nobles** married their children into other rich and noble families. Young men married at about twenty-three, women at about twenty. They often promised to marry each other when they were very young – marriages were most often arranged by the parents.

Villagers

Villagers had a limited choice when it came to marriage. The smaller the village they lived in, the smaller the choice. People did meet and marry outside the village, but most partners came from nearby villages, if not the same one. Respectable villagers mostly married among themselves, as did **labourers**. There were exceptions to this rule, but they were few. Men usually married at about twenty-nine, women at about twenty-eight.

Family sizes

Everyone who could, from rich nobles to farm labourers, followed the same pattern of having children.

The gaps between the first two or three children were very small. This was to make sure enough children were born who would live to inherit their parents' property. After the first three children the pattern varied.

If there were two healthy boys, then the family might slow down and leave a bigger gap before the next child. If there were no boys they would probably have more babies quickly, hoping for at least one boy. The average family had four or five children. But there were huge variations. Some families had none at all, some families had just one. On the other hand, there were some families, especially poorer ones, that had eight or nine children.

Source A

A Tudor cradle, designed to keep babies out of draughts. As many as one in every ten babies died in Terling village in Tudor times. Girls were more likely to die than boys.

A picture of a Dutch woman spinning, painted in 1530.
All women were expected to marry if they could. They
then had to look after the house and children.

9 Houses and homes

Landowners

Landowners had big houses. Some were built from local building materials. During the reign of Queen Elizabeth a lot of landowners built new houses that had more rooms and were more comfortable. If they really wanted to show how important they were, and if they could afford it, they had these houses built from brick or stone that was not made locally and had to be brought in by cart.

Farmers

Farmhouses varied a lot. Some were very grand. Well-off farmers tended to have large farms. They had lots of animals and servants too. The houses had two floors, with several rooms on each floor. There was enough space for the family and servants to live separately. Smaller farms were like labourers' cottages. They might only have two rooms, one for the family and one for the animals.

Labourers

Labourers usually lived in one-room cottages. Often they had to share the room with the animals, building a wicker dividing wall to keep them at one end of the room.

Source A

Houses built in wooded areas use a lot of wood. In open farmland they use as little wood as possible, and fill in with woven sticks and mud or clay. Some places use chalk. In Wales they have reddish stone. In some places by the sea they use crushed seashells and fishbones mixed with mud. Many farmhouses now have several rooms upstairs and downstairs. Windows are covered by **wicker** strips, which used to be filled with polished horn or bone. Now glass is so cheap that almost anyone can afford to use it.

Written by William Harrison in 1577 in *A Description of England*. Harrison wrote about the way Tudor people lived, including their houses, food, furniture and dress.

Source B

A wooden trencher (plate). The hole on the right at the top is for salt. Most ordinary people ate off wooden plates and drank from wooden mugs. If they could afford to, they bought a pewter plate or two for best.

A farmhouse, from a Flemish calendar printed in 1520. Notice the windows, which would be wicker strips, not glass (see Source A). The animals are kept in a separate room at the end of the farmhouse.

10 Shopping

Where did they shop?

Country people shopped at **markets** or at village shops. Most villages had a baker and a butcher. There were also travelling salesmen who carried butter and cheese or fish around the villages. But these people charged higher prices than markets and their food was often less fresh. There were also pedlars, travelling salesmen who sold everything but food – combs, ribbons, tin whistles, buttons, toys and even the latest songs and story-telling pamphlets from London.

What did they buy?

Landowners sent their servants shopping. They needed to buy very little food – their lands provided vegetables and fruit. They kept animals for meat, and could hunt wild animals too. Many big houses had their own **fishponds**. They ate fish on days when eating meat was banned for religious reasons.

The servants might go to the market to buy new cooking pots or expensive foods such as spices, salt and sugar. They were more likely to go to the markets in the big towns and pay with money. Landowners bought things like clothes themselves, often going to London to have their clothes made for them. They might also buy pewter or gold plates or luxuries like clocks in London.

Villagers grew most of their own food. They might go to market for fish and things they ran short of, such as cheese and butter. They seldom bought expensive things, so mostly shopped at the local village market, which sold everything from animals to lengths of cloth. They bought pots, pans, knives and tools from the local **blacksmith**. They bought bowls and spoons from the local carpenter. The growing number of poor people in the countryside could not afford to shop at all. They had to beg for food or live off wild plants and animals.

Source B

Villagers at markets like the one below, painted in about 1600 by the Dutch artist Jan Bruegel, sometimes used money like the coins above. Sometimes they **traded** the things they had for the things they wanted.

Large towns have weekly markets, which sell everything people need. Small towns and villages have them less often. A bushel in one place is very unlike a bushel in another – so people are being cheated. Also, smaller markets are full of people buying poultry, eggs, butter and cheese not for themselves, but to sell at a profit at larger markets or even in London.

Written by William Harrison in 1577 in *A Description of England*.

11 Eating and entertaining

Food

Farm **labourers** mostly ate barley bread and cheese. They also ate bacon or salt pork and chickens or geese that had stopped laying eggs – but not every day. They hunted wild animals, such as rabbits. They did not often eat fish on meat-free days, just home-grown vegetables. They might have a fruit tree in their garden. They drank mainly home-made beer or milk.

Nobles had several sorts of meat for their dinner each day. They could choose from chicken and goose, lamb, beef, pork and also animals they hunted, such as deer. They ate wheat bread, several sorts of cheeses and a wide range of fish, vegetables and fruit. They also used far more flavourings – salt, pepper, sugar and spices, all very expensive. They drank wine and beer.

In between came more ordinary people. They had more choice of food than the labourers, but saw such things as sugar and spices as luxuries.

Entertainment

People in the country made their own entertainment. They danced and made music by singing and playing musical instruments. The rich hunted, others went fishing. Many people swam in warm weather. In bad weather they stayed indoors and played games with cards or dice. Entertainers sometimes came to the villages. There were actors, acrobats, jugglers and fire-eaters.

Dangerous pastimes

The Tudor government passed laws against some pastimes usually because they caused fights, or involved betting, as local court records show.

1569, High Laver, Essex
There were games played, including riffling and bowls, that caused loss of money to many people, mostly the young and servants. Within two days some lost more than their year's wages.

1592, a Lancashire village
An **alehouse**-keeper was fined for having no licence to **trade** and allowing games, including 'bowls, bull baitings and cockfights in which many people lost more than they could afford'.

Even some unbanned sports could be dangerous:

1572, Moulsham, Essex
Tom Hewys and Will Egham were wrestling 'for sport and without malice' when they fell heavily. Hewys hit his head hard and died the next day.

Source A

A Tudor gingerbread biscuit mould. Ginger was very expensive. Most people would not make biscuits like this except as a Christmas treat.

Holidays

People did not have holidays as we do now. They did not work on Sundays, but they had to spend a lot of time at church. They also had the day off on **holy days** (special days in the church calendar). Easter and Christmas were holy days. There were also a lot of holy days celebrating **saints**. On holy days, people could have fun. Sometimes they had special food. There was always a lot of eating, drinking and dancing. Often they put on plays about the lives of the saint whose day it was.

A Carnival on the Feast Day of St George in a Village near Antwerp, **painted by Abel Grimmer in 1603. Some villagers are acting out the story of St George and the Dragon. Others are dancing, eating and drinking. There are some covered stalls selling things. At the back of the picture actors have set up a stage (surrounded by a red cloth).**

Source B

12 Health

Keeping healthy

In some ways, country people were luckier than townspeople, especially the poor. They had more fresh air and better food. They were more likely to have clean water from springs and streams. They were not so crowded together. **Contagious diseases**, like the **plague**, were less likely to arrive or spread as quickly. But plague could strike and wipe out whole villages. Not all wells and springs had clean water. Many houses were damp and draughty. Everyone had to cope with the problems of bad **sanitation**.

Care for the sick

Country people had less choice of who to turn to for help when they were sick than townspeople did. Only the rich could afford to send for a doctor from the town. Most women had their own collection of herbs and knew a few **cures** for simple things, like headache or toothache. For more severe illnesses, villagers had to rely on local people. The landowner's wife often knew about cures and kept herbs in her home. Visiting and helping the sick was one of her duties. Most villages also had someone living there who knew a lot about cures and to whom everyone went when they were sick.

Source A

For head, sinews and eyes:
Roots: acory, peony, iris mandragora
Herbs: sage, betony, marjoram, rue, thyme, eyebright, fennel, vervain
Seeds: peony, aniseed, fennel
Flowers: rosemary, sage, betony, waterlily

For stomach and bowel:
Herbs: sea wormwood, garden mint, costmary
Spices: ginger, mace, pepper, cavaboe

Some cures listed by Lady Grace Mildmay in the 1580s. Many people used cures like these. Lady Grace took cures more seriously than most landowners' wives. She made them in far larger quantities and also made cures that needed large amounts of expensive ingredients, like gold.

Source B

A pestle and mortar, used by Dr Hall of Stratford in the 1590s. These were used to crush herbs or spices to make medicines.

1 />

Source C

I *Crithmum marinum.*
Rocke Sampier.

3 *Crithmum Chryſanthemum.*
Golden Sampier.

A page from John Gerarde's *Herball*, printed in 1597. In Tudor times, books became easier to print and cheaper to buy. This meant more people could use herbals like this, as long as they could pay for the book and were able to read it. It would still have cost more than a **labourer's** yearly wage.

Magical healing

In 1552, Bishop Latimer said, 'A great many of us, when in trouble or sick, run hither and thither to witches or sorcerers, whom we call "wise".' Certainly many of the men and women who gave out herbal cures also suggested cures that sound like witchcraft today. Prayers and chants were often used. In a time when everyone believed in God, it was reasonable that they should expect a prayer to work, if God wanted it to.

Elizabeth Cracklow

Elizabeth, from Adderbury, Oxfordshire, was 'well known' in 1546 for curing dislocated limbs. She held and moved the arm backwards and forwards while her husband prayed over it.

Ann Green

In 1564 Ann travelled in north-east England. She admitted that she used magical cures. These included curing pains in the head by boiling a piece of the patient's hair in their urine, then tossing the mixture on the fire.

GLOSSARY

alehouse   somewhere where beer is brewed and sold

ambassador   a person sent by one monarch to another monarch to sort out a problem: sometimes ambassadors lived in a foreign country and went to Court there regularly

autobiography   what a person writes about their own life

beggars   people who ask for money or food

blacksmith   a person who heats and shapes iron to make tools, horseshoes and other metal things

clergyman   the person who takes the church services

common land   land which everyone in a village is allowed to use

contagious disease   an illness that is easily spread from person to person

Court   the monarch and the people who live and work with him or her

courtier   a person who lives and works with the monarch

cures   medicines or ointments to use when you are sick

enclose   to join together several strips of land and surround them by a hedge or fence

fishponds   ponds to keep fish in made by changing the way a river runs

flax   a plant grown and spun to make linen cloth

gentleman   a man with an income between £500 and £700 a year

graze   to eat grass and other wild plants

hemp   a plant grown and twisted together to make rope

hire   to pay someone to do a job

holy day   a special religious day. People did not have to work, but went to church instead.

industries   lots of people all working together to produce one thing

ironworks   a place where iron ore is dug out of the ground and turned into iron to make tools and other things

labourer   a person who works for someone else doing work that does not need special training, like digging

lease   an agreement made between the owner of a piece of land and another person who pays to use the land for a period of time

lute   a musical instrument with strings, like a modern guitar, but more rounded

Henry VII		Henry VIII
1485	1509	

manor   an area of land which is all owned by the same lord of the manor. It can be small, just a few fields and a village, or much bigger.

market   place where people from the countryside could go on a particular day to buy and sell things

miller   a person who runs a windmill that grinds wheat and barley to make flour

noble   a person who comes from an important family

plague   a sickness that was also called the Black Death. It was spread by fleas that lived on rats and was usually fatal.

potter   a person who makes jugs, bowls and cups out of clay

provisions   things a person or animal needs – food, clothing etc.

sails   the parts on the top of the windmill that look like a wheel. They stick out from the mill to catch the wind and as they turn they work the machinery inside.

saints   people who the church says have done something especially brave for their religion

sanitation   keeping things clean and healthy, good disposal of rubbish and toilet contents

stubble   the stalks of wheat, barley or other grain crops left after harvesting

tailor   a person who makes clothes

tenants   people who rent a house and/or land, paying the landlord with money or work

trade   buying and selling things or (as used on pages 15 and 25) swapping things you have too much of for things that you want

wicker   woven twigs or reeds

will   a list that people make of what they want to happen to all their property (money, land and possessions) after they are dead

Money
12 pence (d) in a shilling (s)
20 shillings (s) in a pound (£)

dward VI | Mary I | Elizabeth I

47 1553 1558   1603

INDEX